WHEN DARKNESS COMES

Saying "No" to Suicide

WHEN DARKNESS COMES

Saying "No" to Suicide

Angerona S. Love

INSIGHT SOLUTIONS, LLC

Copyright © 2010 by Angerona S. Love
Insight Solutions, LLC
FIRST EDITION

Neither the publisher nor the author is offering professional advice or services to individual readers. Any issue regarding a reader's physical or mental health requires consultation with an appropriate, licensed medical or mental healthcare professional. Neither the publisher nor the author shall be liable or responsible for any damages or loss allegedly arising from any words contained in this book.

Book Cover Design by Kathryn Marcellino
www.marcellinodesign.com

Book Cover Photo by Christine Davis

Love, Angerona S.
   When darkness comes : saying "no" to suicide / by
Angerona S. Love. -- 1st ed.
   p. cm.
   LCCN 2009941679
   ISBN-13: 978-0-9825865-0-1
   ISBN-10: 0-9825865-0-7
   ISBN-13: 978-0-9825865-1-8
   ISBN-10: 0-9825865-1-5
   [etc.]

   1. Suicide--Prevention. 2. Suicide--Prevention--Anecdotes. 3. Depression, Mental.   I. Title.

RC569.L68 2009   616.85'8445
                         QBI09-600218

All rights reserved. No part of this publication may be reproduced or transmitted in any form or by any means, electronic or mechanical, including photocopying, recording, or any information storage and retrieval system, without permission in writing from the publisher. Your support of the author's rights is appreciated.

Printed in the United States of America

For Duffy

March 16, 1967 – September 9, 2008
My love, my friend, and my teacher.

Acknowledgements

First, I'd like to thank Bob Rashkin, Bill Harrison, Dave Abt, and David Dashev. You are all instrumental in my still being alive.

Next I'd like to thank Cheryl Simpson for being such a loving friend and helping to take care of so much for me this past year.

To Dr. William Romanos, Jr., thank you for believing in me. Without you, I would not be where I am.

To Tim Andrews, Robert Clayman, Pat Wener, Josh Burrough, Cheryl Rashkin, Samantha Rashkin, Matt Buell, Bob Scharr, and Tom Antion, thank you for your kindness, your friendship, and your generosity of spirit.

To Michael Cohen, Director of Center for Brain Training, www.CenterForBrain.com, and Dr. William "Terry" Ganaway, www.GanawayCounseling.com, thank you for your unwavering support, wisdom, and perspective over the longer haul.

To Andrea Polcyn, thank you for the email I still carry in my purse.

To Stuart Rooney, www.RooneyImports.com, thank you. You know why.

To all my clients and patients, thank you. You give me purpose. You keep me strong.

Table of Contents

Preface 11

I Am 14
Failure 17
Copycats 21
Better Off 24
Suicide Hotlines 29
Flowers 32
Showers 36
Food 39
Animals 43
Bob 46
Bill 50
Maybe 53
Ten Minutes 56
Clouds 59
Sleep 62
Spring 65
Escape 68
Tapestry 71
Future 75
Attempts 78
Living Lies 81
Time 85
Vitamins 87
Music 90
Bodies 93
Choice 104

Afterward 107

Preface

Numerous resources exist for people who are feeling suicidal. However, for those of us who are in despair and hurting, those resources take too much energy to find, they take too much energy to read, and they take too much energy to process.

I traveled to the depths of despair and anguish and, more than once, tried to end my life. These short stories are what helped me. I hope, more than anything, that they help you. These chapters are not grounded in psychiatry or mental health best practices and standards; they are simply the small morsels I grasped onto to try and get through the days.

Suicide creates a vicious vortex of turbulent, gut-wrenching emotions for the loved one's left behind. My world was inexplicably shattered the day I arrived home to find my Dearest Love's body. It is from having gone through the excruciating pain of his suicide, and subsequently becoming suicidal myself, that this book exists.

People say taking one's life is cowardly or selfish. I do not agree. There are just as many reasons for it as individuals, and there are no ways to stereotype or judge another's pain, despair, anguish, and desperation.

At some point, people who have lived through suicide's suffocating grip become happy they are still alive. In sharing parts of the year I desperately wanted to die, I walk the Medicine Wheel back to life. With every healing product created to help others, I mend another piece of myself as well.

Like most who survive and later thrive, I feel blessed that I did not pull the trigger, that I did not hang in my garage, and that I did not combine a toxic mix of pills and dig for the blood deep in my veins. My dance with death ended, and a new life began.

This book is not a magic pill. There are no easy answers and no pat words that can nullify and eradicate the powerful, deceiving, and manipulative energy of the suicidal voice. My hope is that these words will put some additional tools in the toolbox and that the choice to wait will become a little bit easier knowing you are not alone in your pain.

Every moment of life is a step towards healing. Please hold on when you think can't another minute longer. The desperate suicidal wave will be followed by a crest of comparative peace. The crest will not be easy; it will be more bearable.

Please grit your teeth and hang on a little longer.

Please wait.

Please live.

An excerpt from my journal shortly after my fiancé died by suicide.

Sept. 21

I am having a difficult time coping. Dear God, I am feeling suicidal myself. Externally I am composed. Internally I can barely breathe and feel like Munch's "The Scream."

I Am

"I am suicidal."
"I want to die."
"I have run out of reasons to stay alive."
"I don't want to be here any longer."
"I can't do this anymore."

All of these I said, but they weren't true. The language is important.

The truth was this:

I felt suicidal.
I felt I wanted to die.
I felt I had run out of reasons to stay alive.

When I was in despair, I was both confused by and ashamed of who I had become. The woman I knew was smart, radiant, kind, autonomous, positive, cheerful, and keenly aware of her thoughts and actions. The shell that stared at me in the mirror was dark, despairing, sad, anguished, manipulative, clingy, negative, and needy. I no longer knew myself, and what I saw, I despised.

When the tunnel of suicide closed around me, I also believed I was the tunnel. It was innate to my being, as if the tunnel had swallowed me from the inside out. My distorted mind offered no way out of the self-hatred, except to kill my body and end the pain.

The pain was all-consuming, terrorizing, and torturous. I was controlled by my emotions and, in my mind, I was the same identity as the pain. I couldn't see that the words "I am" were larger, greater, and more complex than my need to stop the anguish. My pain was not me. Your pain is not you.

In small moments of self-kindness, I began to separate "I feel" from "I am." In that separation, I allowed the tiny, flickering life force a little more access to air. By changing the language, I took important bits of power back from the deceptive suicidal voice in my head. I took a step towards healing.

The terms "I am" and "I feel" are completely different landscapes. Both feel like crap. "I am" perpetuates the dangerous illusion that the delusional, suicidal voice is truthful and permanent. "I feel" allows some separation and subtly reinforces the temporariness of the turbulence.

You deserve patience and love, no matter your perceived failings. Right now, in this moment, you feel pain and may believe you are pain. Right now, you need a reason to hang on, to believe there is a way out other than suicide.

You feel depressed. You feel suicidal. You feel hopeless and out of control.

Feelings are not facts. Stay alive.

Give yourself room and time to feel differently.

Carl Jung wrote, "You are not what happened to you. You are what you choose to become." I don't feel I can become anything.

Failure

You are not a failure because you are broke.

You are not a failure because someone broke up with you.

You are not a failure because you have lost your job.

You are not a failure because you didn't get a promotion.

You are not a failure because days, weeks, or months of unopened mail sits on your table or desk.

You are not a failure because you hurt someone else.

You are not a failure because you are getting divorced.

You are not a failure because you feel you hate your parents.

You are not a failure because your kid yelled that they hate you in an argument.

You are not a failure because you have a mental illness.

You are not a failure because you have any illness.

You are not a failure because you feel no one understands you.

You are not a failure because you did not get something you wanted.

You are not a failure because someone told you so.

You are not a failure because you feel you have no friends.

You are not a failure because your grades suck.

You are not a failure because you are unexpectedly pregnant.

You are not a failure because you are unable to have kids.
You are not a failure because someone treated you poorly.
You are not a failure because you lost money.
You are not a failure because you are addicted to drugs.
You are not a failure because you have grown older.
You are not a failure because you are not old enough.
You are not a failure because your house is a mess.
You are not a failure because your life is a mess.
You are not a failure because you have lost a youthful appearance.
You are not a failure because a youthful appearance is all you feel you have.
You are not a failure because someone told you that you aren't good enough.
You re not a failure because you disappointed someone you care about.
You are not a failure because you disappointed yourself.
You are not a failure because you believe yourself to be.
You are not a failure.

I have failed at more than most people ever try. I have reigned supreme at false starts and abandoned projects. I have felt like a failure deeply. I have felt "not good enough" for most of my life. I still do.

Not having the energy to get dressed in the morning just propelled my sense of ineptitude and hopelessness.

When I first became suicidal, I considered taking my gorgeous Harley Davidson Softail Deluxe to a deserted road at night, going faster than I'd ever gone on two wheels, then laying it down and hurtling myself along the asphalt.

It was, of course, a foolish plan. Any number of things could go wrong, and the only thing guaranteed was that I would hurt myself beyond recognition.

When I sank further into despair, I could not imagine wrecking my beautiful bike for my hopeless existence. I wasn't worth her destruction. Neither could I imagine wasting a bullet on myself or a piece of rope that could otherwise be useful. Every inhalation felt like an act of theft. I believed more deeply in my awfulness than anything else.

I do not know exactly what turned the tide from ebb to flood. I just know that it happened. I know it can happen for you.

I also know that, as awful as you feel and as much of a failure as you may think you are, it isn't true.

You are not a failure. Stay alive.

Even if it is true, stay alive.

I HATE THE PAIN OF HIS CHOICES. I HATE HOW I FEEL RIGHT NOW IN THIS MOMENT. I HATE THAT I AM STILL HERE.

Copycats

Suicide was always something that happened out there somewhere, far away from my life.

On a beautiful, September Tuesday, I came home to find a note carefully placed four feet inside the front door.

"I know no one will understand this decision…"

My Dearest Love had shot himself in the head. Discovering his body crumbled my foundation. The mental home that held my world views, my judgments, and my realm of possibilities crashed down violently on top of me, and it was almost a year before I could see through the debris.

My fiancé's death brought the world of suicide, the reality of suicide, and the visceral pain of suicide from the jurisdiction of unstable, substance-abusing actors, rock stars, authors, and artists into my yard, my bedroom, my mind, my nerve endings, and my cells.

As I sank further into despair, suicide became more and more seductive. It moved from co-star to leading role, from nightmare to reality. Being forced to live through his suicide somehow rewired my brain and put me at risk for my own.

It is well known in the mental health field that one suicide can prompt others. Those who have lost a loved one to suicide are at *extremely high risk* of completing suicide themselves. I was almost one of those statistics.

Your completing suicide sets the stage for others to follow you. Your fatal suicide changes the emotional and mental makeup of everyone who knows you. Your suicide opens the door for others to consider suicide as a possible solution to their problems.

Most people who attempt suicide are loving, kind, generous, and sensitive people who become overwhelmed and overcome by agony. We cannot recognize how much pain we might cause in others. Suicide is not selfish; it is sheer desperation that falsely claims there is no other answer.

Do not give suicide the power to permeate the lives of those who know you, those who might succumb to their own despair. Give yourself, and others, the option of staying alive.

You may not believe you have anything to offer. Choosing to continue living through each unbearable moment is enough right now. It is the most important thing you can do.

I AM MORE AND MORE LOST. THE PAST TWO MONTHS HAVE BEEN UNBEARABLY HARD. I SO VERY MUCH WANT TO LEAVE THIS LIFE AND JOIN MY LOVE. I AM BIDING MY TIME. I WILL DISAPPEAR, I JUST NEED TO FUNCTION UNTIL THEN. OF COURSE, I AM NOT FUNCTIONING WORTH A DAMN. I AM IN A STATE OF EXHAUSTED ATROPHY. I CANNOT EVEN WRITE. MY SADNESS, MY LETHARGY, MY DESPAIR, MY OWN INTERNAL DEATH IS TOO GREAT. I HAVE ALREADY DIED. I JUST WAIT.

Better Off

A common illusion among those of us who are suicidal is a core belief that our loved ones will be better off without us gunking up their lives. This is false, misguided, and absolute bullshit. This is the suicidal voice talking, and it is not rational.

The aftermath of the suicide of my Beloved hurled me to teetering on the knife-edge of death for months. The fallacy that anyone will be better off without you must be corrected. And I mean right now.

The suicidal voice distorts reality into a twisted, garbled, contortion of lies. This insidious idea that our loved ones are better off if we are dead is perhaps the worst falsehood of all. It leaves complete and utter anguish in its wake, a wake that ripples out and magnifies among hundreds, and even thousands, of lives.

It does not matter how broke you are, how addicted you are, how despairing you are, how alone you think you are, how awful you believe you are as a human being, how altered and crazy your sense of life is, or anything else.

The people who know you will not be better off if you kill yourself!
You will not be doing them or yourself any good whatsoever!

If you are contemplating suicide, you owe it to yourself and those around you to educate yourself on the damage you will leave behind. You are not an exception to this. Your death will negatively impact more people than you can ever imagine, and it will positively impact no one. The inescapable emotions felt by those left behind are wide-reaching, gut-wrenching, and awful.

If you choose to complete suicide your loved ones' constant companions will be anguish, guilt, sadness, despair, bewilderment, anger, physical pain, the feeling of going crazy, forgetfulness, lack of focus, lethargy, anxiety, self-hate, worthlessness, remorse, difficulty breathing, nightmares, insomnia, inability to work, regressed behavior, self-doubt, incompetence, clumsiness, numbness, constant questioning, and suicidal thoughts. These thoughts and feelings will consume your family and friends for weeks, months, or even years. Some of these thoughts will never go away.

If you think this won't apply to you, you're wrong. The American Psychiatric Association rates the stress of the loss of a loved one to suicide as equal to time spent in a concentration camp. Your suicide is not exempt. Other people's insides will shred to raw confetti at your death.

Your life insurance is not worth the pain of your death. Your mental illness is not worth the pain of your death. Your feelings of being a failure are not worth the pain of your death. No matter what is so wrong in your life, nothing is worth losing you to the people who love you or even just know you.

If you think no one cares about you, you're being falsely led by the deceiving suicidal voice.

- Your family and friends will find themselves incessantly defending and explaining your death to most people they talk to. The general public's insensitivity to those left behind after a suicide is a constant, wretched reality. People they don't know will ask them how you died, why you died, who found the body, and what happened. They will be subjected to incessant ignorance and judgment about your decision.

- Someone you care about, whether parents, a spouse or partner, siblings, friends, or colleagues, will be scapegoated for your death, blatantly or covertly. That person, and others, will accept the blame for your suicide, feeling they should have done more, said more, or been more. That intense and aching journey of failure and martyrdom will be torture for months or years.

- The people close to you will experience problems with trust, intimacy, safety, and security. Their foundation will crumble, and they will lose faith in themselves, in humanity, and in the world.

- The person who replaces you at work will walk into a stigma that will stick with him or her as for as long as he or she is at that job.

- Your friends, whether many or few, will ache for your pain. They will experience most of the feelings above and wonder what they could have done differently.

- People you've dated will be deeply saddened by your loss and will revisit every detail of their relationship with you in an effort to examine whether or not they might have contributed to your thoughts.

- Wherever you live, someone will have to clean up your belongings, and perhaps your bodily remains, traumatizing them forever. Someone will move in. Your suicide still will be present in your home, to the new occupant, and to the neighbors around you. Your suicide will not go away until everyone who knew you moves away from the area.

- The people you work or go to school with will question how they could have helped you.

- Even your mail carrier will never again come to your mailbox without remembering that you died by suicide.

I could fill pages with the repercussions of your death on the people around you. Even if you don't feel it right now, your place in the world matters.

Recognize the voice of suicide for what it is: destruction and pain. It is not you. You need to stay alive.

ANOTHER DAY. Jumpy, anxious, sick of myself. I THINK I CAN STAY ALIVE TODAY. PLEASE SOMEBODY HELP ME WITH THAT. I HAVE TO GET THROUGH TODAY. Have to get through today.

Suicide Hotlines

I pick up the phone. I put it down. I pick up the phone. I put it down.

I pick up the phone and dial the number. I don't hit "Send." I put it down.

It is 11:30 at night. I do not know when it got dark. I have been sitting in the chair for an unknown period of time I cannot remember. The darkness outside is in sync with the darkness in my being. I need help. I need help right now, and I am afraid.

My computer monitor glows in front of me. The National Suicide Hotline Number, 1-800-273-TALK (8255), hangs in its pixilated box at the top left corner of my screen.

I do not know what to expect. If I make this call, will police show up at my door in 15 minutes? Is my identifying information going to get put in some databank somewhere? Is this going to hurt my ability to get health insurance? If I admit I am suicidal, am I going to be thrown in a psych ward?

All these questions make me antsy, and I pace in my living room and stare at the phone. I cannot decide if it will become my enemy or my friend.

I do not have the gun in my hand. A noose does not hang beside me. I have not yet taken pills. I am within an hour of killing myself, not seconds.

I dial again and preface the phone number with *67 to mask my own number, deluding myself that this meager protection is any defense against whatever system I am about to enter.

The woman who finally answers the phone after the automated information finishes is nice. She patiently listens to me ramble about my situation and directs my attention to some practical, nuts-and-bolts questions. We talk for perhaps ten minutes.

I hang up the phone after thanking her for her time. I still feel suicidal, but the edge is off. The anxiety level in my chest that previously stifled my breath and felt out of control has been alleviated. I believe I can get through the remainder of the evening alive.

No sirens wail in the night, and the cops do not show up at my door.

I made several calls to the Suicide Hotline when it was late at night, and I was feeling most suicidal. The operators provided varying degrees of comfort and, as to be expected; on occasion I hung up feeling frustrated and misunderstood. On these nights, my aggravation kept me alive. I did not want my last conversation on earth to be annoying and unfulfilling.

Other times, I went to sleep feeling that someone else in the world understood how I felt and was, at that moment, wishing me well.

It is okay to have nothing to give to yourself. Please reach out for help and talk to someone. It's there for you. You do not have to go through this alone.

How is it possible to recover? I really can't believe how painful this is.

Flowers

Filling my days was a torturous task. Every morning when elusive and erratic sleep drifted to wakefulness, despair sucked me into its vacuum.

"Dear God, how am I going to get through this day?" I would think as my eyes focused on the ceiling above me.

Every day, the span of conscious hours seemed an interminable length of time. An entire day was a personal marathon that left me exhausted, foggy, brittle, weak, and emotionally shredded.

To combat this, I drank. I longed for the soothing numbness that would allow me to coast through the next twelve hours in a state of semi-coherency. The marginal drunkenness often ended with nightly plummets and frantic phone calls to a compassionate friend because I was so desperately close to death's clutch.

In an effort to postpone the start of my inebriation, I walked around my yard before I started drinking. At some point in the morning, I stepped from my utility room, out the back door, and into the ever-brightening, south Florida sunshine.

I paused beside the parched, coconut-lined, three-tiered planters filled with herbs on either side of the back door, rolled the leaves of the dying sage, rosemary, oregano, and basil between my fingers, and inhaled the sublime fragrance. The gritty sandstone pavers, cool from the night air, massaged the soles of my feet.

From there, I walked the length of the patio into the back corner of the yard where the hammock hung before my fiancé, Duffy, killed himself. This small corner, holding the potting bench covered in grime, the orchids, and a few random plants confirmed the neglect I would see in the rest of the yard.

I continued past the fountain and around the detached garage to the terraced vegetable garden. Next, I meandered past the fruit trees and then around the remaining long side of the yard. During that walk, I gave attention to every single plant and flower. I noticed the tiny, light green shoots of new growth two millimeters long. I took in slight nuances of leaf color. I tracked patterns of mottled green and yellow.

Occasionally I would even be prompted to fill the water pail and douse the parched plants with life-nurturing water.

I felt a miniscule glimmer in my throat or abdomen when I detected a forming bud or realized a flower would bloom the next day. I collected seed pods, knowing that I might or might not be alive to plant them. If I chose life, I knew I would want more flowers.

These walks around my small plot of yard usually took an hour and a half. I often did not have the energy to water or care for them. Invariably, the noticeable brown edges and withering leaves provoked a cacophony of negative conversation in my mind about how horrible and useless a person I was.

The plants that died received teary, earnest apologies for my ineptitude and forced me to stumble on a vision of my home if I killed myself. No one would live here for a while, and all of it would die. I envisioned my little cottage near the ocean surrounded by dried, wilted, dying plants that had once been so beautiful only because I chose to abandon them. This image further pained my already-shattered heart.

Even if I didn't think I had any reason or right to live, I didn't want to kill the 6,750 square feet of earth I called home. While, in my mind, it was reasonable for me to die, I did not have the right to kill all these beautiful flowers, delicious fruit trees, or exotic tropical bushes.

These plants kept me alive in spite of myself because I felt they were worth more than I was.

I don't always have the energy to water them when they need it, but they still provide me solace and beauty when I feel myself falter. They have helped bring me back to living.

LOTS OF CRYING THIS MORNING. COLD WATER ON HANDS. IN A FOG.

Showers

Depression made small tasks like brushing my teeth, washing my face, and getting dressed seem insurmountable. My skin was a mess, my hair hung limply, and my posture was so poor that a deep breath was physically impossible.

After my morning walk around my yard and my first or second White Russian, I would sit at my desk and determine how much energy I had to dole out for the remaining twelve or fifteen hours of the day. On good days, I tried to accomplish three tasks. Some days, getting dressed was as much as I could manage.

I viewed showers with trepidation, peeling off my clothes with economy to save my limited energy for something more crucial. I avoided the mirror, not wanting to see the pockmarked jaw, lined face, uneven skin tone, expanding waistline, or deadened eyes.

I stepped into the bathtub watching the dirty, first footprints linger on the bottom as I shuffled around the small space. Warm water bounced off my skin. Although my tightly-bound muscles pretended to ward off further escalation of despair, the hot water poured over me and crept through my guard to loosen and relax them. Then the sobbing would start.

I usually ended up crying in the shower.

This relief challenged and scared me. As my body eased, so did my mind. A flood of pain would rip through my psyche, and tears were inevitable. And yet, there is also something supremely comforting about crying in the shower. The tears are total – internal and external – and the soothing cascade of water cleanses on more levels than just the physical.

When I shut off the water, I felt inside-out as if I couldn't tell my insides from my outsides. As I roughly dried myself with a towel overdue for a wash, the slightly mildewed smell returned the hollow shell to the outside and the chewed up core of me to the inside.

I particularly liked the way I felt after a shower. I liked the scent of soap on my skin. In my darkest moments, to "like" anything was a major accomplishment. So even though I often cried in the warming gentleness of the water, showers became a small respite from my pain, even if, at the same time, it was exacerbated.

I AM BARELY EATING, AND INTERNALLY I FEEL BUTCHERED. HOW IS IT POSSIBLE TO HURT THIS MUCH?

Food

I am a foodie. I love food. It is one of my greatest sources of pleasure. Except when I was depressed and suicidal.

After Duffy died, I borrowed food. Almost everything I ate came back up within minutes. My deep grief and sorrow at his suicide wreaked havoc on my body as well as my mind.

I recovered my ability to eat as weeks turned to months, but lost all sense of pleasure. I became a grazer filling a void. As I became more entrenched in the pervasive grip of suicide, I hadn't the energy to eat, nor the desire.

Meals for he and I had been wonderfully intimate events. We cut and diced together. Side-by-side, we stirred and tasted, lifting spoons to each other's mouths, smiling with anticipation. We regularly lit candles and ate in bed. We poured glasses of wine, danced to music, and had great conversation. We prepared picnics for the beach and took off on our motorcycles. Mealtime was magic.

After his death, every bite of food further reminded me of infinite, immeasurable, inconsolable loss.

The mangos on my tree started to ripen and turn golden. Huge clumps of mangos ranged from green to red to yellow to gold. They were beautiful and succulent.

I allowed them to fall and litter my yard with their sweetness. I stared at them from my desk as if foreign beings and watched the flies buzz around them excitedly. Their life force was too great for my own, and they acted as a kind of repellant. My apathy for them only served as another reason to beat myself senseless over my complete worthlessness as a human being.

Then one day, I happened to see one fall out of the corner of my eye. I saw it drop at the same time I heard the resounding "Thump" as it hit the ground. I stood up from my desk and went outside to pick it up.

It was surprisingly heavy for its size, and the warmth of its sun-drenched skin heated my palm and sent tingly nerve responses up my arm.

I walked into the kitchen and sliced through the tough skin with a small paring knife. The flesh inside dribbled delectable fluid over my fingers and into the sink.

The internal organs that had felt dead for so long began to awaken from their hibernation. Jolts of excitement shot up from my stomach as the scrumptious mango perfume infused itself into my being.

I raised the mango to my lips and bit into it without even trying to cut it from the pit. Juice covered my lips and ran down my chin. The flesh was warm, honey-scented, and scrumptiously sweet. It had been months since food had tasted so delicious. I scraped at the bits of flesh and sucked my fingers of every last drop.

Then I went back out to the tree. I stared at it for minutes trying to decide what to do. Despite having eaten from this tree for four years, it felt unfamiliar to me in this moment. With my Dearest Love's suicide, everything in my life had since been divided into "Before" and "After." I was still learning how to be in "After Duff."

In the end, I thanked it for its gift and picked another mango.

After eating a second mango, I realized that enjoying food again could be a possibility. But not if I were dead.

ALL MEANING HAS DISAPPEARED. THIS IS TERROR NO ONE TALKS ABOUT. I AM MY OWN MURDERER.

Animals

As ashamed as I am to write this, at my most despairing, not even my wonderful dogs and cats were enough of a reason to stay alive.

I was too deep in the tunnel to recognize how much their lives would be altered as a result of my death. Nor was I able to comprehend how confused they would be or how much their situation would change for the worse.

My neighbor would take them and love them. At the same time, she has a small house, a small yard, a dog of her own, and no fence. The reality is that my death would have been difficult for my friend and all the sweet animals.

Luckily, my most despairing moments came in waves.

I wasn't cognizant of the hardship to the animals if a wave came while I was away from the house. Perhaps I was out driving and would have to pull my car into a parking lot because I suddenly had no idea where I was going or why I was driving. Perhaps I was in a shop or restaurant, conversation around me forced to the background as the suicidal roar in my head increased to painful decibels.

In these moments, when their worried, benevolent faces were not immediately visible to my consciousness, I felt they would be fine without me.

Fortunately, I was most often at home when a tsunami of desperation overtook me. If I gave in to those moments and leaned my head on my desk, moved to the bed, or sat on the floor, my dogs would surround me with love, licks, and shedding brown and black fur. They patiently sat with me as I clung to them for solace.

In those moments, deserting them by suicide was Option Two instead of Option One. In those moments, I was safe.

The act of feeding them, petting them, and refilling their water bowl forced me to perform a task. Their dependence on me created the only schedule in my life, and because mail sat unopened on my kitchen table for months and I could barely eat, their care was the only act of normalcy I had.

Even at my worst, if I looked at my girl dogs clearly, I knew I could not leave them. However, at the darkest part of the tunnel, the suicidal roar blocked them out, and I focused on planning my death.

Planning my death was not the same as performing my death, and the wave would pass. As much as I really wanted to die, my mission became staying alive through the darkest moments instead of putting the gun in my mouth, hanging myself in the garage, taking pills, or driving across the Intracoastal bridge for a final, late-night swim, all of which I tested.

If I allowed it, the concerned and loving looks in my dogs' eyes could quiet the internal screaming when I needed it most.

EVERYTHING IS A BLUR. IT IS TAKING EVERY OUNCE OF POWER TO STAY ALIVE. I TRULY AM IN ANGUISH.

Bob

Help can come from surprising places. My aloneness was consuming and absolute. My father had died leaving me with no family, my fiancé had died, I had lost the wonderful family I was going to marry into, my father's wife of 21 years had abruptly stopped speaking to me then moved from their home without letting me know, and with rare exception, my closest friends were over 1000 miles away. The two friends who lived close to me had no idea how to help me and, in response, understandably distanced themselves.

One of the days I was most despairing, I edited some previously-written notes to friends with final thoughts and information about how to more easily settle my affairs and wrote a public note for the police. I printed them out and lay one copy on my cluttered desk. I addressed and stuffed two envelopes with the other copies and made the 40-foot walk to the mailbox.

I was too deep in the tunnel to think. My actions were automatic, stilted, and my mind had already mostly left my body. It was mid-afternoon, and I was very close to being ready to die.

I lay on my bed, my upper body propped up on pillows, the loaded revolver in my mouth. The steel gray, matte metal was cold, uncomfortable, and heavy on my lower jaw. My upper teeth rested on the ridged site at the end of the gun, sending unpleasant jolting prickles through the nerve endings of my upper jaw, like biting into chocolate ice cream. My eyes started to tear up.

"Don't think about it. Just pull the trigger," I told myself. Deep in the core of me, I knew this was the wrong choice. I was so tired, so sad, and could not, in any capacity at that moment, find a single thing to live for.

A small quiet voice in my head said, "Call Bob."

I paused, puzzled for a moment. Bob was a friendly acquaintance. Three months prior, I had briefly talked with him and his wife while downtown getting something to drink. This made no sense.

"Call Bob."

The barely audible voice was insistent. I dutifully slipped the gun between the mattress and box spring and slung my legs over the side of the bed. I could barely see. Darkness closed around me in a putrid swamp.

"Just do it." Another louder, deeper voice argued for complete annihilation. A few seconds to grab the gun, ram it in my mouth, and squeeze the trigger, and it would all be over.

I waffled. I could feel my internal pilot light dimming, becoming drenched in the murkiness of despair.

It was this miniscule light, this tiny shred of life force that propelled me to the other room. I dug into a grocery bag of office supplies and sat hunched over rubber-banded stacks of business cards searching for the light blue one I hoped would save me.

As dead as I already felt, that tiny flicker of life fed the diminutive voice that said, "Call Bob."

I found his business card and flipped it over to read the handwritten cell phone number on the back.

"Bob? This is Ange. May I please have five minutes of your time?" I sounded far away from myself, pinched but composed.

"I'm with my grandson," was his reply.

The pilot light faltered in an icy wind, and the guillotine slammed shut. I became dizzy as I felt myself swooshed into a cyclone of fearful resignation.

Then he said, "I'll be there in twenty minutes."

"No. That's okay. I'm sorry, I just..."

He cut me off. "I'll be there in twenty minutes."

His crusty, grumpy exterior protects a decent and loving heart, a heart that had compelled me to call him.

I was embarrassed. Someone I barely knew was going to see me at my absolute worst, my most vulnerable. But he was coming, and relief oscillated through my body.

I put the gun back into its holster, hid the note on the desk, gathered the letters from the mailbox, and sat on the bed waiting. Bob was coming.

Hope and help can come from the most unlikely of places. I was lucky to listen to that small voice of self-preservation. We all have one, and even if it suggests something seemingly crazy, this is the voice you need to listen to.

The suicidal voice is loud, all-encompassing, resounding, and absolute. The voice of self-preservation is soft, tender, compassionate, quiet, and hurting. That warm, gentle voice will save and support you as you begin the arduous, laborious, and intricate climb to health.

Against all logic, I called Bob because that voice told me to. I do not know how he knew I was in trouble except, possibly, that I had never called him before.

His arrival defended me from death that day. His humanity saved mine when I had none left to offer myself.

He and I, we saved my life.

PLEASE — SOMEONE -- SOMETHING — HELP ME RESTORE MYSELF. I CANNOT EVEN BREATHE.

Bill

The desperate phone call to Bob gave my life a temporary reprieve. I, however, had not changed. The insidious allure of suicide was just as pervasive as ever.

I continued with my planning, determined that the additional week or two would simply allow me to clean up a few more personal details, not prevent my suicide. I rationalized that the extra time would just make it easier for the person I had made the executor of my estate.

Monday, during a late-night, drunken phone call to my friend, Bill, I did more than allude to the fact that I was in trouble. I cried about my inability to take any more and about all the pain, loss, and tragedies of the prior year. Indeed, it had been a year whose degree of pain, loss, and tragic events was nearly unfathomable.

I rambled on about updating my will, getting property records in order, and overnighting him some documents in the next few days.

Tuesday, Bill was on a plane to Florida.

Bill convinced me to do an inpatient "vacation." Bill quietly stayed present. Bill did not try to fix me. Bill let me know I was loved, no matter what.

Bill is not perfect. The people who love us never are. We cannot count on them to save us. We must save ourselves. However, when they try, we must honor the voice that stands up for life. The voice that begs for a few minutes more. The voice that stands for love, no matter how flawed.

Bill, like Bob, gave me more time.

The day will come when I don't wake up wanting to die. I'm just not sure when that will be. I want to feel just a few minutes of relief. I want to be rescued from my pain. I want to trust my ability to make decisions again, to not doubt myself.

Maybe

We seem to think that, when we start to feel better, we will have a linear journey on an upward path. Several times I had a decent few weeks or month only to become a crying and despairing suicidal mess, yet again.

Not only did I wallow and wonder if I would ever escape suicide's hold on me, it also taxed my counselor and my friends. I felt increasingly alone and increasingly without options.

In a good moment, I wrote in my journal, "Maybe it is remotely possible I won't always feel this way."

I stopped and looked at the sentence. I felt completely hopeless, empty, and emotionally constricted. I had no faith in the statement. Even the remote possibility that anything might be different only seemed like it could be true for somebody else. I felt trapped in a dark, dense tunnel, and my own mind was my enemy.

And yet, the statement stuck. On days when I found myself propped against the wall staring at the shower curtain wondering how I was going to make it out of my bathroom, the statement would come to me.

"Maybe it is remotely possible I won't always feel this way."

I ended up writing this statement on sticky notes and posting one on the refrigerator, one on the bathroom mirror, and one at my desk. I also kept one in my purse in case I had to go out to buy milk or dog food.

This was not a cheery mantra or affirmation. I never said it five times while smiling at myself in the mirror.

I whispered it quietly to myself in desperation as tears spilled from my eyes. I tried to hear the words in my mind as I grappled for control over the whirlwind confusion telling me to end my pain.

This statement did not always make me feel better. In fact, on rare occasion, it could make me feel worse. If there was even a remote possibility, why couldn't I get there?

Also on rare occasion, it could make me angry. Anger came as a relief. It was something other than absolute despair and could give me energy to cook something to eat or wash dishes.

Most of the time when I read this it gave me hope that I could someday feel hope. Maybe not today, and maybe not tomorrow, but it was possible.

That remote possibility helped keep me alive when I felt I couldn't make yet another phone call to the few people I was afraid of alienating even further.

Everything is just so overwhelming! Getting dressed, checking mail, everything. I have to go through this. I have to stay alive. I have to stay alive.

I am so scared! I am falling apart. Falling completely apart.

Ten Minutes

I am frenetic and frightened. I cannot withstand the suicidal voice any longer.

85% of me wants to die
12% doesn't care
3% wants to live

I cannot do this another moment longer. I cannot see, I cannot hear, and my pain is unbearable. Not another moment longer.

I can feel the raggedness of my breath and struggle to form a sentence in my mind.

"How long can I hold out?" I ask myself.

The suicidal voice reaches hysteria, and a massive storm further annihilates my tenuous mental grip. The clanging craziness of the executioner in my mind is immense.

I find myself clutching my cell phone with shaking fingers, frantically pressing buttons to find the alarm.

"Ten minutes," I hear my voice say. "I can commit to not hurting myself for ten minutes."

I find the alarm but now can't remember what time it is. Frustrated, I switch to the main display. I say the time aloud over and over so I don't forget it again while I toggle back to set the alarm.

I focus all my concentration on successfully adding ten minutes to the present time. The alarm is set. I double-check it. I cannot afford a mistake. I wait. The tempest rages.

I stare at the cell phone waiting for the minutes to change. I doubt myself, believing ten minutes is too ambitious. The noise in my head disembowels me.

I carry the phone to the bathroom and rest it on the back of the toilet. My eyes search for something calming, and I reach into the shower, pull out the bottle of coconut shampoo, and inhale the fragrance. After several inhalations, I replace the shampoo and open pomegranate lotion, thrusting the bottle under my nose. In my desperation, I forge my way through perfume, shower gel, soap, and random toiletries.

The alarm rings.

I set it again. Ten minutes. The fury in my head subsides slightly. I can control this, if only for a few minutes at a time.

Days and weeks went by for me five, ten, or on good days, twenty minutes at a time. In those few moments, I dissected the contents of my bathroom and kitchen looking for pleasant things to smell. I played music. I shuffled cards. I pulled out a guitar and clumsily fumbled with chords. I looked at flowers. I squinted up at birds flying across the sky.

I did anything to make the time pass. I did anything to stay alive.

It worked. Ten minutes at a time.

Unsettled. Guilty. Hard to keep my equilibrium. Hard to keep anything.

Clouds

I stepped through the French door onto the deck and walked five paces to the outdoor sofa. I turned and sank into the cushions, full of despair and lacking in energy.

This was another small escape from my misery. The shell I had become rarely ate, slept poorly, and couldn't think. My eyes were dry and scratchy, my face pinched, and my skin pocked from lack of care. But I could watch the clouds glide past, sculpting themselves into any shape my imagination could envision.

I lay back, adjusted my body against the shifting cushions, and gazed upwards, tuning in to the carnival above. The shapes came effortlessly. An elephant head formed, seemingly like magic, and lazily morphed into an alligator. Whales turned into dogs, and I watched profiles of men with fedoras, witches on broomsticks, and lounging women.

The overhead theatre seemed to hold lessons for me as the clouds dissolved and reformed before my eyes. I was barely aware of the breath in my lungs and nostrils, of cars driving by, or of dogs barking in the background. I just watched the clouds. The suicidal sadist sometimes quieted to a dull, throbbing ache in my brain, and I had a few minutes of peace.

On particularly bad days, none of them looked like anything. On these days, I would lie in bed and beg for death or my life back.

The amorphous, puffy glimmers of white, silver, yellow, blue, and pink helped me pass time, pass days, and find some small bit of whimsy in a dark world. Finding shapes in these soaring clouds gave me some connection to elusive life when I felt I had none left.

If I remembered to look up, I almost always received a small gift from nature. Clouds were nonjudgmental witnesses of my pain and continued to drift gently along, sometimes soothing me with their grace.

Woke up this morning under the same oppressive energy, the anger, the sadness. The nightmares have gotten so bad, I'm afraid to go to sleep. No alcohol for three days now. No sleep either. Sigh.

Sleep

Sleep does wonders for mind and body. Unfortunately when in the ravages of despair, sleep is often fitful, restless, erratic, and fraught with nightmares that inconspicuously lead further into the suicidal trance.

My whole body constricted into itself from exhaustion. I had no peripheral vision and felt cloaked in foul-tasting fog. I was constantly cold. I became desperate for rest and would sob at my inability to succumb to it. Sleep became a sociopathic lover, taunting me with bliss and rejuvenation that remained stubbornly evasive.

Eyes stared at the ceiling, out the window, into eyelids, and at the clock. I wrestled with covers, changed sleeping positions, and tried alternate sides of the bed. I moved the clock so I could convince myself I may have gotten some sleep and hadn't watched the night pass by one minute at a time. That just meant I got up regularly to look at the cell phone plugged into its charger in the other room.

I played the well-proven, hypnotherapy CDs I had made for my business when life was happier. I played other meditation CDs I had bought to compare them with mine. Nothing worked.

My fiancé had struggled with sleep as well, waking numerous times in the night to listen to the radio, fix a drink, sit outside, or play guitar. At the time, I did not know how much lack of sleep supports the downward spiral into the suicide dance.

When I could fashion several solid hours of slumber, I awoke with a better outlook, not good, but not suicidal either. Relief flooded my body, and I knew I could manage a greater part of the day without feeling I was falling apart. I could chew food and taste it. I could hold a coherent conversation without other people sounding like they were underwater.

Sleep is vital. If you aren't getting the rest you need, please get help. Do not trade temporary insomnia for permanent sleep. Insomnia and depression can pass. Death is forever.

Lots of anxiety.
Lots of fucking anxiety.

Spring

Spring to summer is a pisser. Everybody else gets happy, plans trips, and starts exercising. Couples hold hands, people smile at each other in passing, and drab-colored coats get moved to the back of the closet.

My expectations were too high. I wanted to stop crying. I wanted to take my body off and be able to breathe without pain, even if just for one hour.

I couldn't figure out how to do that through living. The problem with suicide is that it would kill all of me, including the small part of me that wasn't quite sure it wanted to die.

That small part of me that "wasn't quite sure" wanted to enjoy the new blossoms, the birds chirping, the warm clear nights, and the light spring rains. The rest of me wasn't able to enjoy anything and overwhelmed my mind with desperate thoughts of ending the pain.

The beauty of spring and summer, with all its new growth and accompanying optimism, only helped the suicidal voice increase its decibel level, insistent that death was the way out of misery. I needed additional vigilance during these times in a body that felt too tired and decimated to live.

Spring was confusing and my despondency absolute. I felt more and more isolated as I watched people around me become more productive and forward-looking.

To my dismay and embarrassment, I became more manipulative and needy, and less honest. I held self-pitying grudges that reinforced my perceived pathetic existence. I turned my self-absorption knob to high. I could not pull myself out of my mental and emotional prison.

I'm not sure how I stayed alive as spring became summer. I'm not sure how the miniscule part of me that "wasn't quite sure" managed to carry the heavy, burdensome weight of the part that wanted to die.

The standard misconception is that more suicides happen around the holidays. That isn't true. More suicides happen in the spring and early summer than any other time in the year. I didn't understand that before I was suicidal. Now I do.

Spring is hard. Get through spring.

The melancholy and low energy continues. I want off this ride.

Escape

Spiritual views are individual, complex, and important.

Some people believe we go to Heaven, Purgatory, or Hell. Some people believe we incarnate as a higher or lesser being. Some people believe in a metaphysical spiritual existence without human judgment or organized monotheism. Some people believe we just decompose, and that's it. Some people don't know what they believe.

I believe we have a soul and that we live multiple times. I believe that, when we die, we take ourselves with us – our foibles and our strengths. Death is not a permanent getaway from who we are. I think we still have to deal with our shortcomings and our mistakes after dying.

While I do not believe in Hell, I believe people who deliberately end their lives early need to do important spiritual work to counteract the repercussions of the life they didn't fulfill. In my most risky suicidal times, I was okay with that. I was willing to pay any karmic interest rate necessary to alleviate my debilitating and complete despair.

That was the irrational voice of my pain talking.

Life is not a board game with "Get Out of Jail Free" cards in every deck, and at no point is that more obvious than when we would give anything to escape the jail of depression. Our very lives become a negotiable commodity.

When I didn't think about any kind of afterlife, suicide seemed an easy option...my only option. However, when I considered what would happen after I killed myself according to my spiritual beliefs, it seemed imprudent to flagrantly give up this life, despite how desperately I wanted to end it. It seemed more a prolonging of pain, just in a different form.

In the moments when suicide was slightly less imminent, I saw the illogic of trading my seemingly unbearable, known pain for an unknown pain that might be worse and last longer.

When I thought about dilemmas of the soul, I questioned whether or not I wanted to burden mine with such a poor choice made in a human body. Do I or don't I? Is it worth the cosmic repercussions or not?

I wavered and waffled constantly depending on how I felt, which was in and of itself, erroneous and unsound.

Questions concerning escape and soul journeys often have no place in the spinning whirlwind of the suicidal mind. We are too busy clenching our teeth against the onslaught of pain that already feels larger than the universe to consider the soul.

I found that a few moments of quiet consideration of the soul could give me the wistful wherewithal to make it through the next few minutes of suffering. The raging sea would subside momentarily, the sails would stop clanging, and I could massage my hands and fold my body in temporary reprieve.

Dying is not an escape. Guard and be gentle with your soul.

I JUST NEED TO STAY FOCUSED ON THE LOVE. THAT IS WHAT MATTERS MOST.

Tapestry

The tapestry needs you.

A few weeks after Duff died, I had a powerful dream. As I floated in the sky, I saw a massive, shimmering, magnificent tapestry. Dozens of somethings zipped and hovered around the tapestry. Some religions might call these angels or fairies. I do not have a word for them, but they were obviously some kind of celestial beings.

I could clearly see where Duff and I were woven into the intricate and beautiful design, rich in color and glistening with gold and silver. I was enraptured by the exquisite image before me of lives intertwined.

My eyes drifted further up the tapestry. There, the deliberate, self-inflicted slashing of his thread left the one end frayed and dangling. The colors darkened, and foreboding crept in.

Suddenly, ragged patches, threadbare spots, and gaping holes replaced the beauty that would have been our journey together. Deep chasms in the tapestry stood testament of life undone, experiences unfulfilled, and whispers unrequited.

My thread, my little sliver of sacred essence, skirted around these shredded gaps as if knocking scared and barefoot on doors in the night. This tender, blessed, single thread sought out solace and wholeness and found none.

Small seraphs cried as they tried to patch the places his violent death had left tattered and bare. Their tiny hands rested lightly on the abraded edges with both compassion and sadness.

When I awoke, I was sobbing. I knew deeply in my core how large a loss his death was to the world and how many people he was supposed to impact who would never know him. I knew the holiness of every soul on earth. I knew in the vibration of my cells how valuable life is.

Of course, in my own despair, I selectively forgot this dream. When I remembered, I deluded myself that my contribution to the world did not matter all that much.

Yet, if I got quiet and allowed myself to go deeper than the experience of despair, I knew that I did matter, and that even if I didn't want to acknowledge it, my self-inflicted death would leave the same holes and damaged, ragged patches in the tapestry.

Stay in the tapestry. We have no idea how many people will benefit from our existence.

Perhaps your stopping at a yellow light prevents the person behind you from being killed or killing another by running the red. Perhaps something you casually mention causes a colleague to change a career and live a dream. Perhaps you notice someone trying to break into a neighbor's home as you pull into your own and save jewelry belonging to a long-deceased grandmother or a computer that holds both personal and important information.

Any of these induce positive change for generations, impacting countless people to come. One small or large kindness can truly affect thousands, as can tragedy.

If you choose to make that final choice now, you leave gaping holes – wounds in the tapestry that need to be mended and smoothed.

I felt so isolated and so insignificant and so trapped when I was in the well of darkness that I could not imagine being more than a cut thread and a tidy knot, an annoyance in the overall scheme. The echo in the suicidal tunnel reverberated my despair and self-loathing back to me in a deafening roar.

I saw my place in the tapestry as more accountability I didn't ask for. I saw it as a burden, and I, quite frankly, didn't give a damn about my responsibility to it.

Except that I did. Suicidal people tend to be really good, sensitive people who are hurting. We do care. We do not want to let the world down, but our pain has become so consuming, we see no other choice.

Continue weaving. This tapestry of life is a picture larger than we can comprehend. The dark greys, blacks, browns, and other putrid colors that make up the current cloth will give way to purples, then blues, then greens, reds, and pinks. Vibrant glimmering threads are coming. This period of darkness can give way to light. The tapestry still needs you. It needs all of us.

I WOKE UP TODAY IN ANGST AND ANGER. THERE IS SUCH A DICHOTOMY ABOUT TRYING TO MOVE FORWARD AND BEING IN ABSOLUTE DESPAIR.

Future

When darkness fell around me, the word "future" simply meant two 'u's, an 'f', a 't', an 'r' and an 'e' arranged on the landscape of my mind in a way that read "f-u-t-u-r-e". It meant nothing more.

"Future" was something nebulous, something completely detached from my experience. When people spoke of the future being happier, I looked into a Black Hole, a void. I would listen to their words and nod my head, but secretly, I was confused. I could not even fathom two days from now.

Well-intentioned people asking me to have lunch next week brought about anxiety attacks. There was no "next week" for me. There was only now and now sucked.

Getting through the present moment took so much of my energy that any reference to the future left me feeling like I had to decipher a foreign language, some kind of code I wasn't privy to.

Friends and acquaintances trying to help me feel better enthusiastically speculated about the future, reminded me about the Law of Attraction, and stated how much more improved I would be if I would just buck up and pretend I wasn't so depressed. These comments furthered my isolation and fortified faulty proof that I was better off not being here.

Statements like, "You will get through this" helped. I could define the "this" in whatever way was comforting to me in that moment. As was, "You will be okay."

As soon as a statement defined time, I was lost.

"In a year from now, you'll look back on this…"

I was gone, cocooned in my desperation. For me, there was no such concept as "a year from now". The person might as well have been talking about the next time I travel to Saturn.

The hopelessness caused by an inability to envision a future is part of the seduction of the suicidal voice. The inability to see a future does not mean it isn't there. You will not always feel this way.

Without hope, it is difficult to perceive a future. Without any sense of future, it is difficult to generate hope. The two are intimately and inextricably tied.

You can get through this, and you can be okay. Do not force or pressure yourself about any future right now. Get through this minute, this hour, and this day.

The future is made up of moments. For right now, just get through them one at a time. That is enough. When the moments get a little easier, the scope of your vision will naturally increase.

Get through this moment.

I THINK I REACHED BOTTOM YESTERDAY. I HAVE NEVER BEEN THIS KIND OF SCARED BEFORE.

Attempts

After Duffy killed himself, I needed to know everything I could about what people who lose a loved one to suicide go through, as well as what happens in the suicidal mind. I incessantly tried to make sense of chaos and voraciously read books, articles, studies, and abstracts to feed my morbid quest for methods, statistics, experiences, and demographics.

I had one close-up experience with suicide, and someone I loved died. It was sudden, violent, bloody, destructive, and traumatic.

By chance, in reading about suicide, I read about all the things that go wrong. The more I read, the more I discovered, the more afraid I became.

I learned the reality is much different. I learned the grisly other side of suicide no one talks about. I learned that for every one person who dies by suicide, at least 20 others attempt to die, many of whom require emergency medical care.

I read about gunshot wounds that left people brain-damaged and blind, hangings that left people in comas. I read about overdoses of both prescription and over-the-counter drugs that resulted in permanent damage to organs, drastically affecting people's ability to eat or use the bathroom normally.

I read about paraplegics, quadriplegics, and limbs shattered in jumps from bridges. I read about years of pain and trauma from people who set themselves on fire. I read about women who will always wear long-sleeves so the scars on their arms do not show.

I read about people whose suicide attempts had so damaged their bodies they were unable to attempt suicide again. These people are forced to live in nursing homes trapped in their anguish with round-the-clock care.

If you are seriously considering suicide, you need to know the odds. You need to know the damage you are likely to do to your mind and your body that will follow you for years to come.

You need to know how many people clang their hospital bed rails and scream in frustration and agony at new wounds and permanent damage, in addition to their temporary depression.

You need to know how differently people will look at you as you try to rebuild your life and how long it will take to regain your loved ones' trust. You need to know how different your friendships will be as friends tiptoe around you, get nervous in your presence, abruptly stop laughing at something funny as if they're doing something wrong, and glance furtively at each other gauging every word out of their mouths and the reactions of your facial expressions.

You need to know the price you will pay. You might die, and that ultimate price will destroy the people who love you. However, it's more likely you will live and suffer from organ failure, need painful surgeries, live in a wheelchair for life, have brain damage, or worse.

Educate yourself about suicide. I thought people who attempted suicide died. The reality is it is not quick, it is not painless, it is not romantic, and it is not easy.

I can't remember who I am. I need to. I need to remember who I really am. This shell of a person isn't me -- can't be me. God please, can't be me.

Living Lies

A friend of mine, a psychiatrist, believes that suicidal people don't necessarily want to kill themselves. He thinks they want to kill their old selves.

That may be true. For me, I definitely wanted to die and reunite with all the people I love who had left the Life Journey. I didn't think there was anything left for me here, and there seemed to be a lot Over There, wherever Over There is.

I follow his meaning. Many of us have created lives that aren't what we want. We find ourselves studying subjects in school that aren't what we want to study, we take jobs that aren't what we want for work, we get married to people we might have slivers of doubts about, we shop according to society's fickle whims, and we entrench ourselves in identities that may not fit.

If you have a life you don't recognize or want, give yourself a chance to be who you are. If you've been living someone else's life, give yourself a chance to live your own. It's okay if you don't have all the answers. It's even okay if you don't have any answers. The only mistake that is undoable is suicide.

I lost my father and my fiancé three weeks apart. My fiancé and I were scraping by financially, and we worked together in a budding business.

He was a part of every aspect of my life. We played together, worked together, slept together, cooked together, ate together, showered together, made love together, rode motorcycles together, played guitar together, sang together, gardened together, worked on our old house together, and took walks on the beach together.

I could not fathom living after he died. My entire being shattered into a thousand glass shards that raked at my torso, drawing fresh blood with every breath.

I had no idea how to earn a living without him. I suddenly inherited all the household bills and lost over half the household income. I didn't know how to operate some of the equipment our business depended on, and because we had been so entwined in each others' lives, I wasn't even sure how to take basic care of myself despite having done so for many years.

In short, I was heartbroken, broke, without family to lean on, and the thought of having to put a life back together was overwhelming and incomprehensible.

It took almost a year of dysfunctional and despairing behavior to begin moving forward. I have remembered some of the things I liked to do before he and I moved in together. I have remembered some of my personal pleasures he didn't enjoy. I have released some of the things I thought I really liked, but only did because he loved them.

I have gained significantly more trust in myself, in part because I am trying to build an authentic life that is completely on my terms. This is not easy, nor is living someone else's life.

I am stronger, more centered, and more grounded now. I still have financial qualms, I still have no family, and I still get overwhelmed. I still suck at housecleaning and let bills pile up on the table. I also love my work, can see a future, and know where to get help when I need a tune-up.

Before you make a decision on suicide, give yourself an opportunity to rest. Give yourself time to sit calmly with your pain and listen to your inner wisdom. It might say, "I've fucking had it with this and want to go to a movie." It might say, "I want a pizza with pineapple on it." It might say, "I've always wanted to paint." It might say, as mine did, "It's time to write again."

Whatever it says, this is the voice of healing. This is the voice that will liberate you if you give it space and time to be heard.

My self-doubt is oppressive. How am I going to get through this? How do I ~~mistake this~~ maze for a labyrinth?

Time

Several situations created time for me when I thought I wanted no more of it. Bob, Bill, inpatient care, driving, and especially taking trips all helped me stay on the right side of the strained connection between my life and my death.

Time was the difference between living and dying. Time quietly deliberated with the booming, omniscient voice of suicide and told it to back off.

Paradoxically, time was both my nemesis and my healer. I wanted it to end. I wanted death. I wanted no more minutes, hours, or days of anguish. And yet, time was the only thing that could save me. It kept me perilously balanced on the beam when I wanted to tumble into the abyss. The irony was cruel.

Had I made that final choice, there would have been no healing. Time could not have become malleable, and it could not have changed from enemy to ally. Gradually time shifted my perceptions about myself and a possible future.

If I had made that final choice, I would have lost all options for my life to be different. The minutes that clicked by in interminable misery slowly became my lover and my friend, but only because I stayed here to experience the lurching shift.

The shift will come. Time is the only thing that can bring it.

I am a basketcase. An absolute mess. I need to stop drinking, I really need to stop. I need to do one thing to take care of myself.

Vitamins

I stood at the sink with the small capsule cupped in my right hand. I felt like shit, I was drinking heavily, I couldn't eat, and I wasn't remotely taking care of myself. In a stroke of brilliance and energy, I had decided to take a vitamin.

My left foot curled around my right ankle as I looked at the puke green capsule in my hand regretting my decision. As I considered putting this unpalatable thing in my mouth and swallowing it, my gag reflex retaliated.

"You need to do something," the voice in my head said.

The suicidal roar was strangely silent and, in the stillness, I began to doubt myself. I didn't deserve to feel better. I deserved to die for not stopping Duffy's death. I was a selfish, horrible person. I had nothing to offer. The world would be better off with me gone.

The blustery wind of the suicidal storm in my mind picked up these thoughts and broadcasted them throughout my brain.

My left hand gripped the edge of the counter, and I squeezed my eyes shut. I popped the vitamin in my mouth, tossed my head, and doused my throat with water. My gag reflex kicked into overdrive, and I started to retch. I shook my head, tossed it backwards again, and swallowed.

"That was a lot of drama for a stupid vitamin," said the negative voice in my head.

I, however, felt instantly better. This small act of self-care gave me a tiny sense of success over my suicidal mind.

Vitamins will help make up for some of the deficiencies in diet and uneasy sleep. Spiritually, it is a caring act for a body, mind, and soul in pain. I wish I had done it all the time. I think it would have made a difference.

Take a vitamin. Today.

> STARTING THE DAY SEEMS A
> MONUMENTAL TASK
>   CAN'T WRITE. CAN'T THINK.
> CAN PLAY GUITAR.

Music

I sat on the floor in front of the stereo listening to the same song for the zillionth time. It reminded me of everything I'd lost and further quagmired me in the muck. I felt consumed by my isolation, the sadness in the music, and the uselessness and hopelessness of my existence.

"Why am I doing this to myself?" I thought as I sat curled up in the dark. Even though I hated how I felt, I didn't believe I deserved to feel differently.

Hesitantly, I placed a different disk into the CD player, found the song I wanted, and pressed "Play." This one was more inspirational. It wasn't sunshine and rainbows; I couldn't have stomached a cheery view of the world. It was about overcoming difficulties.

As I listened, I felt myself change. Instead of crying about all I'd lost, I focused on the pain the singer had pushed through. I focused on the beauty in her voice. I focused on the message that triumphing over hardship can be worth it.

The second time through, I found myself softly singing the chorus and swaying with the rhythm. The deep inhalations I took to hold the notes brought oxygen to my beat-up brain, relaxed and nourished my body, and released vitally-needed endorphins into my bloodstream.

The third time through, I got up off the floor and sang loudly enough to hear how badly I sounded. For once, it didn't matter. The sensation of breathing fully for the first time in months was bliss compared to my absolute dejection fifteen minutes prior.

While I was still sad and despondent, I learned that music was a powerful tool if I could refrain from playing the songs that acted like quicksand on my mind and heart. At times that wasn't easy, and I was often tempted to use music to drop me to my knees rather than help elevate me.

Music can nurture the soul. It changes the brainwaves and promotes all kinds of physiological change. A song about fighting back, finding faith, recovering from hardship, or positive change in the world can allow a few moments respite from the constant jack hammering of sadness, strife, angst, and despair.

Playing music took up time. I could distract my mind temporarily with lyrics or harmonies. When I was desperate for ways to get through my days, these short bursts of color were a blessing. I tended to play the same few songs over and over. I didn't have the concentration to flip through disks searching for the perfect 3.5 minutes for my morbid mood.

I rarely moved from my spot on the floor in front of the stereo. No matter how little energy I had, I could hit "Play."

Play music.

Play music that is a little more positive than you feel.

Play it often.

Play it now.

I have just gone back and read this journal. I have made so many bad decisions these past six months. I must choose peace. I must choose spirit. I must stop choosing out of reaction. I must figure out what it is I want. I have no idea.

I have been all over the place these last six months -- each time thinking I was on track when it was all just reaction.

Wanting to die is particularly reaction. I am needed here.

I wish it wasn't true.

Bodies

Bodies want to live. Bodies do not die easily. I have experience.

Five weeks after my dad died and two weeks after Duff died, I somehow regained consciousness in my bathroom. It was dark.

My feet and legs were crumpled under me. Next to me lay an upturned bottle of vodka and several empty packs of sleeping pills.

The next wave of vomit hit the toilet and splattered the front of my shirt, shaking me further awake. My eyes widened with the realization of what I had done.

I did not remember wanting to die that night. I did not remember anything leading up to that moment at all.

For the first time in my life, I jammed my fingers to the back of my throat, forcing myself to throw up for what felt like hours. My sobs mingled with borrowed liquor and semi-dissolved pills in the bowl of the toilet.

My fear wasn't in dying. I had no idea what I had taken or if I had taken enough of whatever it was. I was more afraid of not dying, of going to the hospital, and of ending up severely damaged.

When I began dry heaving, I pulled myself upright, washed my face, brushed my teeth, and collapsed in my bed.

I awoke close to noon the next day. As I drifted from sleep to wakefulness, I became aware of a metallic taste in my mouth. Memory of the previous night flooded my body, and I tried to open my eyes.

My eyelashes were glued shut and crusty from tears. My fingers gently stretched the tender skin under my eyes to release the delicate hairs. My swollen, right eye opened, followed by my left.

I shuffled into the bathroom to spit the acidic taste from my mouth. My throat was raw and bits of blood came out with the saliva that had sat in my mouth overnight. My salivary glands were on overdrive and stringy spittle continued to dribble from my mouth.

My jaw ached, feeling bruised, as did my ribs. My stomach clenched and spasmed as I steadied myself on the sink. I cupped cool water into my hands, rinsing away the residue of the night before.

My own mind was trying to kill me. I felt nothing, no horror, no pain, and the mirror reflected an image only vaguely familiar. Sometime in the night, I had become a hollow shell, an expat of my own body. I felt brittle on the outside and completely empty internally.

That was the first time.

Between the first and second time, I practiced with the revolver, placing it in my mouth or against my temple at least thirty times. I experimented with finger positions on the handle and imagined the results if I pulled the trigger.

I planned. I wrote letters. I prepared my estate. I was consumed with the thought of my death. I saw no other way out. No other option.

Then light started to twinkle at the far edges of darkness. I would like to say that was the end of my suicidal struggle. It's not.

I had finished my inpatient "vacation" and had started to feel slightly better. I was a wispy, pale shadow of myself and spent a tremendous amount of energy to avoid another breakdown. Even though I was still suicidal, I was tired of worrying and disappointing the few people who cared about me and felt their patience wouldn't hold out much longer.

One semi-major setback sent me tumbling towards the abyss again.

Weeks after my inpatient therapy, my partner in a brand new business abruptly quit leaving me to pick up the pieces. I had clung to this business as the only possible hope I had for the future and poured all my physical, mental, and financial resources into it. With its hasty demise, I struggled against avalanching rock, could not gain my footing, and sank back into despair.

Because I had glimpsed the edge of normalcy and, again found myself struggling for breath in darkness, the stifling nature of suicide penetrated even more deeply into my bones. The whiplash-inducing descent sucked me down completely.

After a particularly awful day dealing with my former partner, I showed up exhausted at the 10-bed, residential, inpatient facility that had become my lifeline. I was desolate, barely articulate, and knew I was a danger to myself. I urgently needed to stay the night.

In a necessary and impromptu session, my counselor pointedly proposed I spend a few days in the hospital. I declined, realized the precarious position I was in, and used every ounce of strength I had to pull myself together while in his presence.

He then mentioned possibly Baker Acting me, which would mean three mandatory days in a psychiatric ward, as well as the significant expense and disruption accompanying the involuntary commitment.

The air in the room hung thick as asphalt, and I began counting my breaths. My fear and mistrust were palpable, and my mind screamed in repudiation.

I had just over $400 to my name, and my fledging business had just disintegrated. Already, I could not pay my mortgage and had no source of income. I felt the debt incurred from a Baker Act would push me that much closer to suicide. I needed kind intervention, support, and money, not three days of lockdown. I watched him warily and continued counting to calm my racing heart.

He maneuvered with caution, choosing his words and actions carefully. His speech was metered, and while he acted nonchalantly, his observation was acute. He agreed to let me stay there that night and told me he would be back early in the morning. He also said he would refrain from imposing a Baker Act as long as I upheld my end of our agreement.

I had proven to be a person of my word, even in my darkest moments.

I spent the night without sleeping, and left as soon as the sun turned the sky pink. When he called a couple hours later, I apologized for leaving so early and convinced him I was through the most crucial few hours of attempting suicide.

Over the next few days, my mind became wholly governed by suicide's grip. Although I regularly checked in with him as agreed, I was perfunctory and less than honest.

A week later, I paced the floor at home, leaning to look out the window every time a car went by. I became deeply concerned and moderately paranoid that he would reconsider, and that the police and a psychiatrist would show up at my door with a signed paper to take me away. Each secondhand ticking of the clock was an eternity. I wondered if he was just placating me so I wouldn't run.

I am, indeed, a runner.

I felt so disempowered by the despair of my own body, mind, and heart, that the thought of giving up control of my whereabouts, my food, my clothing, petting my dogs and cats, my music, my ability to drive, and my bed to spend three days in the psych ward of a hospital was unconscionable.

Fear overrode logic and reason.

I ran.

I packed an overnight bag and jumped in my car. I had no idea where I was going and didn't tell anyone I was leaving until I was well away from south Florida. Even then, I only called my neighbor to ask her to watch my dogs and two friends who both lived over 1000 miles away from me and would have a hard time intervening.

My goal was to disappear. I didn't know if that was forever or a few days. Any concept of time slipped from my consciousness. I just drove.

After a decent dinner outside Savannah, Georgia, I headed east. I found myself at a beach 550 miles from my home. My affairs were in order, and my car would be found in the morning. I was ready for, desirous of, and welcomed a drowning death. My senses were hyper-aware; my mind a chunk of wood.

I slipped off my flip flops in the sand about thirty feet from the water's edge, followed by my black yoga pants and a pink t-shirt I was wearing for the first time. I folded the t-shirt neatly. It was new, and the wastefulness of buying a t-shirt, wearing it once, and then dying before it had even been washed crossed my mind.

This small pile in the sand seemed surreal, no longer having anything to do with me. I realized these were the last belongings I would ever see.

The sand was damp and cool on the soles of my feet. My thoughts focused on "The Awakening" by Kate Chopin, and I felt a romantic kinship with generations of women before me. I was not, at this moment, rational.

The suicidal voice beckoned, seduced, and cajoled me into thinking this was for the best. I listened with rapt attention. My life-force pilot light whittled away to a miniscule, blue, pencil dot of a flame.

I stepped into the water and felt the frothiness of the sea. The night was calm, and it was easy to wade out to waist-high water. The gentle swells started to lift me up as I continued traversing the sandy bottom until I could no longer touch ground.

I started swimming. My shoulders stretched as I crawled my way out to even deeper water. I began wondering about the tide and if it would pull me out to sea for the next few hours or push me back to the sandy beach. I rolled onto my back and relaxed into backstroke.

The stars above were gorgeous and seemed to twinkle extra brightly for me that night. The suicide voice took this as affirmation of my choice. I wondered if I would be able to see stars in death.

I was mildly afraid. The sea was so gentle, fluid and swaying, with long swells that rolled through me like music. It was, however, very dark below the surface of the water. My mind danced ominously through possibilities, and getting eaten by a shark was not the death I envisioned for myself.

I swam fully, trying to tire myself out so this didn't last very long.

My mind and my heart were ready. I raised my arms above my head and sank below the surface of the water. I held my breath this time, testing.

I returned to the surface, treading water. My breathing was irregular, and I counted to four on each inhalation to calm myself. Lights twinkled on shore, and I turned my body to face the vast expanse of the Atlantic.

I sank below the surface a second time, opened my mouth, exhaled, and cautiously inhaled a small bit of the sea. The brutally cold, salty water surged into me, burning my throat and nostrils. My eyes opened wide at the pain and were immediately stung.

I coughed and gagged, and the ocean rushed into my orifices. My head shook violently to rid itself of the invasive sea water. Thunderous pounding in my ears disoriented me, and bubbles from my frantic flailing surrounded me. With every retch, I heaved more salty water into my lungs, which constricted and struggled for oxygen.

I was no longer in control and felt myself shutting down. I desperately wanted this to be over and tried to operate my arms so they would continue pushing me down further from the surface. They were disconnected, and I could not move them the way I wanted.

I felt an odd swoosh and a warmth beneath my feet. Against my will, I seemed to shoot to the surface. My body was not going to die.

Above water, my arms thrashed wildly as if I were trying to climb out of the sea. Guttural moans and rasping cries seemed too loud for my body as I choked and gasped for breath. Slightly warm sea water purged and gurgled from my throat with every heave. Each time my head was thrown forward in convulsion, the ocean lapped at my lips, nose, and eyes causing momentary terror as I fought to not inhale more.

I expected the ocean to be raging out of control, as I was, and was surprised she hadn't changed. Her rhythm continued rocking me gently as I floundered on the surface. I needed to regain some strength, but the thought of staying in the water caused panic to spread through my mind and body.

I was in the ocean seven hours from home and had now twice lived through suicide attempts. Coughs wracked my chest, and sea water continued to dribble out of my mouth cloaking my chin in slimy saliva. I looked again at the stars while slowly treading water. I felt turned inside-out, raw, and insignificant.

In a rare moment of wisdom, I had given Bob my gun and knew I wouldn't get it back until I was fully committed to living. I didn't want to slice myself open and bleed to death in the bathtub.

I figured I could hang, but my suicidal energy had completely collapsed. I knew now that my body would not go easily. I wondered if my body would go at all.

Numbness replaced fear. Why couldn't I die?

I felt the ocean tenderly lift me towards shore with each swell, and I began to swim. Slowly. Carefully. Mindfully.

The swells turned to crashing waves. The water rushed over my back, and the swirling sand from the bottom buried under my fingernails. I crawled to shore and rested on my knees and elbows. I was still spitting up hot bits of salty water mixed with bile. I tucked my legs up under me in fetal position, resting my forehead on my cupped hands. My fingers became a sieve through which my grief and anguish poured, burrowing into the sand to be healed by the earth.

The etheric scales tipped in that moment, and I felt an energy that was bigger and greater than my misery. I was still just as much a hostage of hopelessness and hurt, but somehow, for just a minute, my essence expanded to hold my misery rather than my misery imprisoning my soul.

I pushed up on my knees and turned over, leaning back on my hands. My body was completely numb. My face stung and my nostrils, throat, and lungs were scratchy and painful.

I picked up a clump of seaweed, formed it into a ball, and threw it into the sea to figure out which way the water was moving. I watched it meld with the ocean currents for a clue to the direction of my clothing and car.

I had spent months complete in my despair and consumed with self-loathing. I had no family, few friends, and no job. I was broke, scared, and, in my opinion, worth nothing. I had to find a reason to live that was larger than my agony.

I had nothing left to lose. I had learned how many people are in pain, what that pain feels like, how many people try or die by suicide, and how many people are left behind shocked by the intensity of the aftermath. I imagined different scenarios in my mind, testing how it felt to share my most vulnerable, intimate, and horrifying moments. It felt oddly exhilarating.

While the nugget for this path had formed soon after Duff died, it had been quickly buried in the ensuing darkness. The vision became clearer as I watched the drifting seaweed and the rhythmic undulation of the ocean. Soft sounds of the sea replaced the roar in my ears.

I didn't want anyone to go through what I had experienced this past year. If I could make a difference, maybe I would believe life was worth living again.

I suddenly realized I was cold and naked. Deflated, I stood, brushed the sand from my cramping body, and walked gingerly down the beach to my clothes.

In my surrender, I knew I would begin to back out of the tunnel and away from the suicidal voice. I knew I would live.

Still, it was not a straight journey. I tested, teased, and thought about suicide daily. For months, I repeatedly stood on the edge of death hoping to lose my balance. I made nooses and hung them from different places in my home to decide which spot would be best. I wrapped my neck with different textures of rope, stood on stools, and gauged the length necessary to achieve fatal results. I researched drug combinations and alternate ways to asphyxiate. I had dreams and nightmares about suicide, funerals, and different versions of afterlife.

While I had mostly stopped drinking, on occasion I would purposely drink too much just to see how screwy my head might get, to see if that night might be the night I died. I deliberately got drunk and played sad songs to see how far over the ledge I would lean.

I engaged in risky behavior, taking walks late at night, being careless with my safety, driving recklessly, and welcoming turbulence on a plane and the possibility it would go down with me on it.

Gradually those moments lost their prominence. Now they no longer exist.

The suicidal voice might always reside in the shadows of my mind. It is now a hoarse whisper. It has taken too much of my life away already. It gets no more.

THE GRIEF OF THIS PIERCES MY VERY
BEING. I NEED TO WRITE AGAIN.
MAYBE IT IS WORTH STAYING ALIVE
FOR THAT.

Choice

As long as you wait, you still have a choice. Once you exercise this final choice, there is no chance to turn back, to undo, to say you're sorry.

The second time I met the man who became my counselor, he walked me out to my motorcycle after our consultation and said, "Look, I'm not asking you to take suicide off your list. I just want you to get it out of the number 1 or 2 slot. Keep it on the list, just move it down low enough that you have other options."

Having the option to complete suicide can always be there. Maintain your choice. Move it down the list.

See www.AngeronaLove.com for more options.

I THINK I'LL STAY HERE. THERE
IS SO MUCH I CAN DO -- HERE.

Afterward

It is late, dark.

Tonight the manuscript is finished. My fingers have played jazz over the keyboard, dishing out dissonance and stream of consciousness in letters versus musical notes.

Dissonance and stream of consciousness are trademarks of depression and despair. When darkness comes, these words defy meaning, becoming a relentless scream in our minds.

I lived. My sincerest hope is that you do too. Your song, your unique voice, matters to the world. Let your voice be heard.

Send me your stories. What keeps you going? What prevents you from making that final choice? What, however briefly, quiets the dissonance of your mind when the darkness overtakes you?

You are my family. All of you whose lives my words may touch. Otherwise, I have none.

When the darkness becomes too great for you to manage on your own, please reach out to someone, to anyone. Let small kindnesses work their way into your core to fight the suicidal voice that is deceptive, malignant, harmful, and wrong.

You need to live. The world needs you. You need you. You need to fight for your life. You are important, and you matter.

About the Author

Angerona Love is an author, speaker, and Applied Suicide Intervention Skills Trainer. She has a hypnotherapy practice in Palm Beach, Florida and offers an online coaching and mentoring program. In addition, she hosts individualized, holistic retreats for people coping with stressful events. Love is dedicated to helping people who are feeling suicidal and those grieving the suicide of a loved one. She is earning a Ph.D. in Jungian Psychology and lives near the ocean with a small menagerie of dogs and cats. For more information, please go to www.AngeronaLove.com.

CPSIA information can be obtained at www.ICGtesting.com
Printed in the USA
LVOW13s2359060714

393077LV00023B/497/P